A New True Book

BABY ANIMALS

By Illa Podendorf

This "true book" was prepared
under the direction of
Illa Podendorf,
formerly with the Laboratory School,
University of Chicago

CHILDRENS PRESS, CHICAGO

Baby robins in nest

PHOTO CREDITS

James P. Rowan—2, 11 (bottom), 20, 24, 26, 29 (bottom), 30 (top) 40, 42 (right), 43 (left), 45 (left).

Lynn M. Stone—Cover, 6 (right), 7 (right), 13 (bottom left), 15 (right), 23 (left and right), 29 (top and middle), 30 (bottom), 42 (left)

Cincinnati Zoo: Janet Ross—6 (left), 7 (left), 11 (top)

Lincoln Park Zoo: Mark Rosenthal—8

Equus Magazine: Bobbie Lieberman—9

Allan Roberts—39

U.S. Department of Agriculture, USDA—4, 45

Smithsonian Institution, National Zoological Park—13

Cover-Coyote Pup

U.S. Department of the Interior: Jim Frates—13

Texas Department of Highways & Public Transportation—43

Reinhard Brucker—15

Louise Lunak—16

Tony Freeman—18

Jerry Hennen—32 (3 photos) 34, 35, 38

Art Thoma—36

Library of Congress Cataloging in Publication Data
Podendorf, Illa.
  Baby animals.
  (A New true book)
  Previously published as: The true book of animal babies. 1955.
  Summary: Highlights the characteristics and behavior of a variety of animal young and distinguishes between those that are hatched and those that are born.
  1. Animals, Infancy of—Juvenile literature.
[1. Animals—Infancy] I. Title.
QL763.P63   591.3'9   81-9938
ISBN 0-516-01605-9   AACR2

TABLE OF CONTENTS

4

SOME BABY ANIMALS
MUST BE CARED FOR
BY GROWN-UP ANIMALS

Many kinds of young animals need help. They cannot take care of themselves. Most of them are taken care of by their mothers.

Baby lambs cannot take care of themselves. They stay with their mothers.

Bat

Vampire bats

A baby bat stays with its mother. It clings to its mother as she flies through the air.

When the baby is big enough, the mother hangs it upside down. She leaves it while she goes to hunt food for herself.

Lion cub

Fawn

Lion cubs need both
their fathers and their
mothers. The cubs need
food and protection.

A mother deer hides her
fawn among tall plants.
This helps protect the
baby from its enemies.

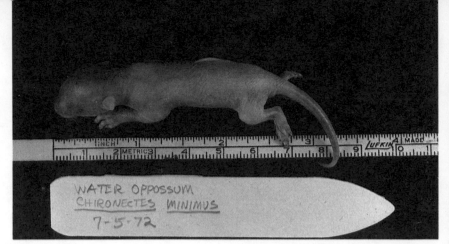

A 16-day-old
water opossum

Baby opossums are very tiny when they are born. They have no hair and cannot see.

Baby opossums live in their mother's pouch. When they are about eight weeks old, they come out. They ride on their mother's back. Now they have hair. They can see.

When kittens are born, they are not fluffy. They cannot see and they cannot walk. Kittens change a lot while they are young.

A colt looks like a grown-up horse. Its legs are wobbly, but a colt can walk when it is only a few hours old.

Very young camels can walk, too, but not very far. Their legs are not strong enough for long trips.

When skunks are a few weeks old, they learn to hunt food. Their mother teaches them.

Bactrian camel

Horse

A baby hippopotamus lives in water with its mother. It rides on her back when she swims in deep water.

Baby rabbits grow up in a few weeks. Then they take care of themselves. Their mother may have another family to care for by that time. A mother rabbit may raise three families in one summer.

Nile Hippopotamus

Fox

Cottontail rabbit

Most foxes are born in April. Baby foxes live with their father and mother in a den. They come out when they are about four weeks old. They are fully grown by September.

Most beavers are born in May. When the young are four weeks old, they begin eating plant food as their parents do. In about two years, they are grown-up.

Most baby bears are born in the winter. They stay in their mother's den. They sleep and they drink a lot of milk.

Black bear cub   Polar bears

The mother brings them
out when they are a few
months old. Then they hunt
for other food.

When bears are about two years old, they are able to look after themselves.

A baby elephant has a woolly coat. Grown-up elephants do not have woolly coats. Elephants are not fully grown until they are about twenty years old.

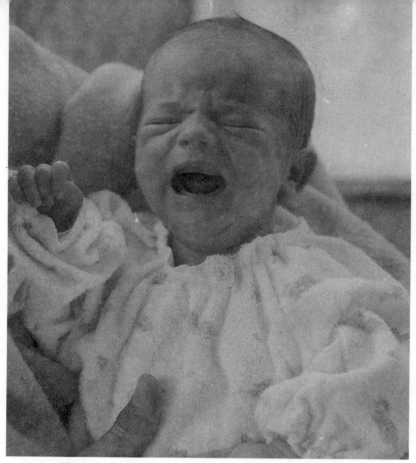

Our baby brothers and sisters need help. They need someone to feed them, dress them, carry them, and keep them happy.

Most of us need our parents until we are grown-up. They give us food, clothing, and a home.

Parents teach us many things and send us to school. They love us and we need that. We love them, too.

Sow with piglets

SOME BABY ANIMALS
DRINK MILK

The babies you have
been reading about
depend on milk for food
when they are very young.

Their mothers' bodies
make milk out of some of
the food they eat. The milk
is stored in milk glands.
The babies nurse the milk
from the milk glands.

SOME BABY ANIMALS
DO NOT DRINK MILK

Some kinds of babies do not drink milk. Their fathers and mothers hunt food for them.

Tiny robins have almost no feathers. They get feathers when they are about eleven days old.

Robins

Goslings of a Snow Goose

Baby geese are called goslings. Goslings have down on their bodies when they are hatched. They get feathers later.

Canada Geese

Their mothers teach the baby geese how to swim. They learn how to find food, too.

Robins and geese are alike in a special way. They both get feathers. Can you think of another way? Did you think of wings? Did you think of beaks? Did you say that they are birds?

Young American alligator

SOME BABY ANIMALS TAKE CARE OF THEMSELVES

Baby alligators and crocodiles hatch from eggs. They can take care of themselves as soon as they are hatched. They will probably never see their fathers or mothers.

Turtles hunt for food soon after they are hatched. They will probably never see their fathers or mothers.

Young insects find food for themselves.

Baby fish hunt their own food, too.

Baby ornate box turtle

Baby loggerhead turtle leaves its egg and heads for water.

A young grasshopper is called a nymph.

Leopard frog

Tadpoles

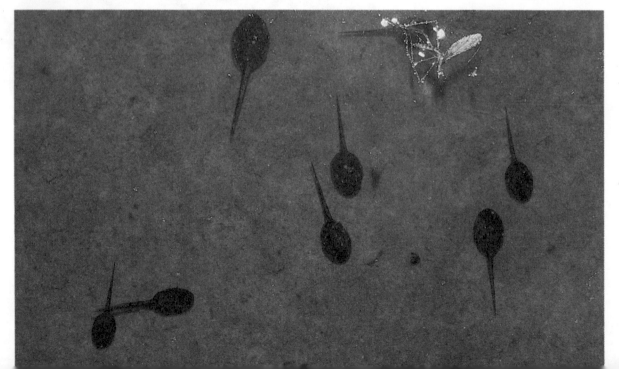

SOME BABY ANIMALS CHANGE A GREAT DEAL AS THEY GROW UP

A baby frog does not look like a frog. When it is hatched it is called a tadpole. Tadpoles can live only in water.

A tadpole loses its tail and gets legs as it grows up. It also loses its gills and gets lungs. Then it becomes a frog. It can live on land now.

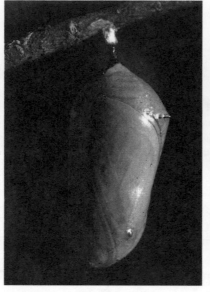

Monarch
caterpillar

Chrysalis

Monarch
butterfly

A very young butterfly does not look like a grown-up butterfly. It is a caterpillar. Soon it will make a chrysalis about itself. Inside the chrysalis it will change into a grown-up.

ALL BABY ANIMALS
COME FROM BIG ANIMALS
LIKE THEMSELVES

Some animals lay eggs. Each egg has an egg cell inside it. The egg cell may grow into a baby animal.

Eggs come in different sizes and colors.

Ostrich eggs are very big. They are as big as twelve chicken eggs. A baby ostrich is about as big as a mother hen.

A hummingbird's egg is very small. It is no bigger than a pea. Think about how small the baby hummingbird must be.

All birds lay eggs. Inside the egg is the tiny egg cell. There is food and a space filled with air inside the egg, too. The baby bird will need food and air as it grows.

Robin nest with eggs

Cardinal nest

An egg cell may grow into a baby animal if it is kept at the right temperature for the right number of days.

Mother birds keep their eggs warm with their bodies.

Robin

Eggs must be protected
from their enemies, too. A
mother bird hides her nest
where it cannot be easily
seen.

A robin must sit on her nest fourteen days before the eggs will hatch.

A mother hen must sit on her nest twenty-one days before the eggs will hatch.

A mother duck must sit on her nest twenty-eight days before the eggs will hatch.

Young red tail hawks, 7 days old

When a baby bird is
ready to hatch, it breaks
the shell of the egg and
comes out. It breaks the
shell with a sharp point on
the end of its beak.

Baby Pilot Blacksnakes hatching

The eggs of other kinds
of animals are kept warm
by the sun. Mothers do not
stay with the nest.

Chacma baboons

Not all animal babies are hatched. Many animal babies are born.

A baby that is born comes from its mother's body. It grows from a tiny egg cell.

The baby is carried inside the mother's body while it grows big enough to be born. Before it is born, the baby gets its food from the food its mother eats. It gets oxygen from the air its mother breathes.

A raccoon kit (baby)

Wisents are European bison.

Raccoon and bison mothers have egg cells inside their bodies. The egg cells may grow into baby animals.

Mother whales have egg cells inside their bodies, too. A baby whale may be as big as an elephant.

Some animals have only one baby at a time. Other animals have more than one baby at a time.

Baby animals are ready to be born at different times.

It takes fifteen days for baby hamsters to be big enough to be born.

It takes nine weeks for baby puppies to be big enough to be born.

It takes nine months for our baby brothers and sisters to be big enough to be born. For a baby elephant, it takes twenty-two months—almost two years.

Chicks do not drink milk.
Calves do.

All babies that are born drink milk during the first part of their lives. Baby animals that are hatched eat many other kinds of food.

WORDS YOU SHOULD KNOW

alligator (AL • ih • gay • ter) — a large reptile with a short, wide snout.

beak (BEEK) — bill; the hard outer parts of an animal's mouth.

bison (BY•sun) — large animal with short horns and fur. The American buffalo is a bison.

breathe (BREETH) — to take in and force air out of the lungs.

caterpillar (KAT • er • pill • er) — the young of a butterfly or moth after hatching from an egg.

cell — the smallest part of a living plant or animal.

chrysalis (KRIS•eh•liss) — a strong case that encloses a moth or butterfly in which the adult grows

cling (KLING) — hang on to; hold tight to.

colt (KOHLT) — a young horse.

crocodile (KROK • uh • dile) — a large reptile with long, narrow jaws.

den — the home of an animal.

depend (dee • PEND) — need; rely on.

different (DIF • uh • rent) — not the same; unlike.

down — fine, soft feathers or hair.

enemy (EN • uh • mee) — not a friend.

fawn — young deer.

fluffy (FLUFF • ee) — soft and light.

fully (FULL • ee) — totally; completely.

gland — a part of the body that stores and releases materials.

hummingbird (HUM • ing • berd) — the smallest bird whose wings move so fast they make a humming noise.

hunt—to look for; search.

insect (IN•sekt)—an animal with six legs and three body parts.

nurse (NERSS)—to drink milk from a milk gland or breast.

ostrich (OSS•trich)—a very large bird which cannot fly.

oxygen (OKS•uh•jin)—a gas which plants, animals, and people breathe.

parent (PAIR•ent)—a father or mother.

pouch (POWCH)—a part of an animal's body that is like a pocket.

protect (proh•TEKT)—keep safe; free from harm; guard.

raise (RAYZ)—to bring up and take care of.

shell—the outer covering of a bird's egg.

space(SPAYSS)—an empty place.

special (SPESH•uhl)—different from the usual or common; unusual.

stored (STORD)—kept.

tadpole (TAD•pohl)—a frog or toad that has just hatched from an egg and lives in the water.

temperature (TEM•per•ah•cher)—a measure of hot or cold.

trip—travel; journey.

whale (HWAYL)—a very large mammal that lives in the sea.

wobbly (WOB•lee)—not strong; unsteady.

wooly (WOOL•ee)—thick, soft hair covering of animals.

INDEX

About the Author

Born and raised in western Iowa, Illa has had experience teaching science at both elementary and high school levels. For many years she served as head of Science Dept., Laboratory School, University of Chicago and is currently consultant on the series of True Books and author of many of them. A pioneer in creative teaching, she has been especially successful in working with the gifted child.

A New True Book

MOON, SUN, AND STARS

By John Lewellen

This "true book" was prepared
under the direction of
Illa Podendorf,
formerly with the Laboratory School,
University of Chicago

CHILDRENS PRESS ™

CHICAGO

Library of Congress Cataloging in Publication Data

Lewellen, John Bryan, 1910-
  Moon, sun, and stars.

  (A New true book)
  Previously published as: The true book of moon, sun, and stars. 1954.
  SUMMARY: A brief introduction to astronomy, with emphasis on the relationship between the moon, the earth, and the sun.
  1. Astronomy—Juvenile literature. [1. Astronomy] I. Title.
QB46.L59   1981   523.2   81-7749
ISBN 0-516-01637-7

TABLE OF CONTENTS

The moon is about 238,857 miles away from Earth.

THE MOON

When you look at the moon at night, it plays a trick on you. The moon looks bigger than the stars. But it isn't.

The moon is much smaller than the stars. It is much smaller than the sun. It is much smaller than Earth.

The moon is much closer to Earth than any star. It is closer than the sun. That is why it looks so big.

Hold a penny close to your eye. It looks big.

Look at a penny across the room. It looks small.

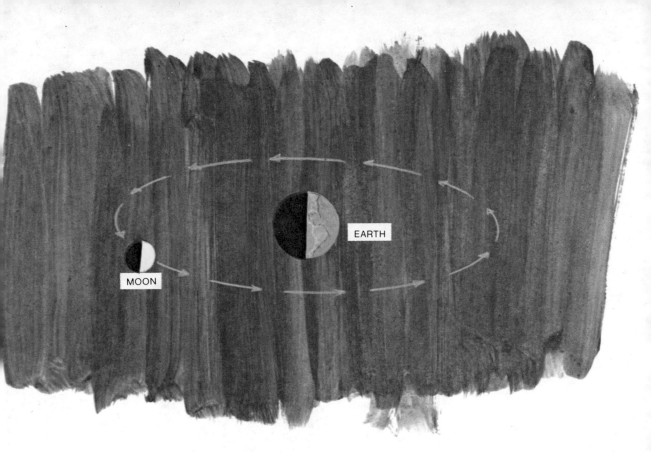

HOW THE MOON MOVES

The moon moves around
the Earth. It makes one
trip in about four weeks.

Craters on the far side of the moon

We see only one
side of the moon. We
never see the other side.
Only men in spacecraft
have looked at the other
side of the moon.

This 19.84-pound moon rock is nicknamed "Big Bertha."
It was brought back to Earth by *Apollo XIV.*

THE MOON IS MADE OF ROCK

The moon looks flat to us. But it is not. It is shaped like the Earth. The moon is made of rock.

People once thought there was a "man in the moon."

The *Apollo XIII* spacecraft photographed the far side of the moon as it went around the moon on its trip back to Earth.

What looks like a "man in the moon" are mountains, and holes, and flat rocks.

There is no air on the moon.

There is no water.

The crew of the *Apollo XVII* took this picture of the moon.

Days and nights on the moon are two weeks long. Days are very hot. Nights are very cold.

If there were rivers on the moon, they would boil in the daytime. They would freeze every night.

There are no plants or animals living on the moon.

Only astronauts have walked on the moon. To protect their bodies from the heat and the cold they must wear space suits. They carry their own supply of air, too.

15

THE MOON IS LIKE A MIRROR

People once thought the moon had fires on it. They thought the fires made it bright.

Now we know the moon is like a mirror. It gets its light from the sun.

We see only that part of the moon lighted by the sun.

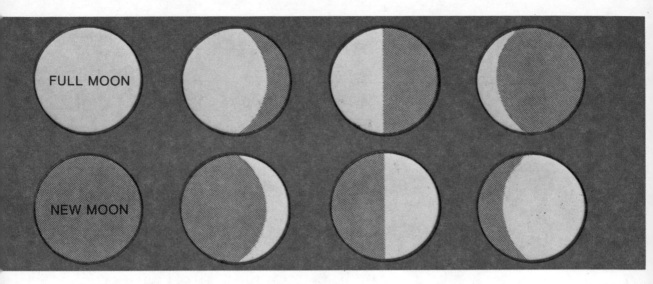

FULL MOON

NEW MOON

When the moon is fully in the light of the sun it is called a full moon. As the moon moves around Earth more and more of its surface is not lighted by the sun. When all of the moon's surface is without light from the sun it is called a new moon.

The rest of the moon is there, but most of the time it is too dark to be seen. That is why the moon seems to change its shape during the month.

You can see how this works with a ball.

18

Let the ball be the
moon. Let your head be
the Earth. Let the light be
the sun. Turn around with
the ball. Do you see the
shapes of the moon?

The ball also shows why we see only one side of the moon. As you turned with the ball, you saw the same side of the ball all the way around.

The moon turns around once while going around the Earth. The ball did the same thing. That is why we see only one side from Earth.

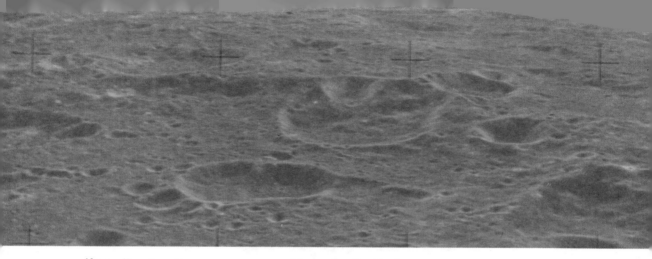

If you lived on the moon you would see the Earth rise every day. This photograph of "Earth-rise" was taken by the *Apollo XII* spacecraft.

THE EARTH IS LIKE A MIRROR, TOO

Spacemen on the moon could see Earth.

The Earth is like a mirror, too. It looked bright when the sun was shining on it. It looked like the moon, but bigger.

The light of the moon comes from the sun. Our daylight comes from the sun, too.

This beautiful shot of the Earth was taken by the *Apollo VIII* spacecraft. The South Pole is in the white area on the left. North America and South America are covered by clouds.

Sunrise in Utah

THE SUN

What is the sun? The sun is a star. All the stars we can see have their own light.

There are many big stars we cannot see. The light has burned out on some stars. Other stars are still bright, but they are so far away we cannot see them.

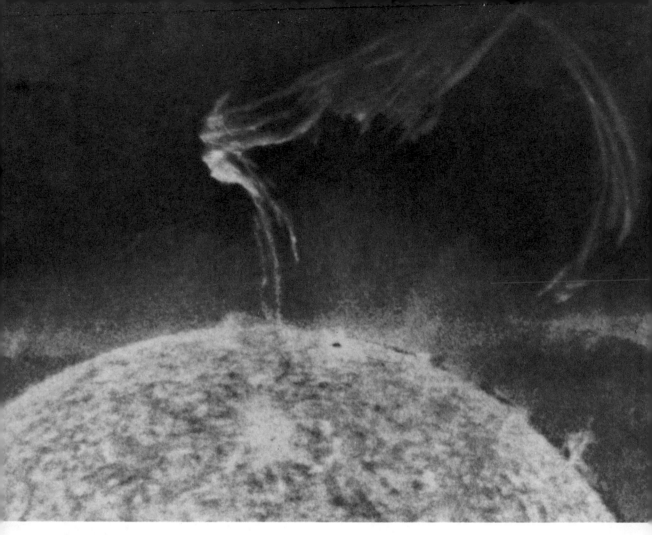

The sun is a burning star.

The sun looks bigger
than other stars because it
is closer to Earth.

26

The sun and other stars we see are very hot. They are like great balls of fire.

The sun is far away. And the air around Earth saves us from the heat of the sun. The air keeps Earth from getting as hot as the moon.

Milky Way
Galaxy

Many stars are in the sky all day. But they are far away.

The sun is closer and its light is much brighter. It is so bright we cannot see the other stars in the daytime.

Part of the time the moon is in the daytime sky, too.

Sometimes it is bright enough to see during the day.

Although the sun is a star, we do not see it at night. At night the sun shines on the other side of the Earth.

If you took a jet at night and flew to the other side of the Earth, you would see the sun.

It would be day there. It would be night here.

Do you know why this happens?

THE EARTH MOVES

Have you ever seen the sun set? It looks like the sun moves down in the sky. But the sun does not move when it sets.

The Earth moves!

As the Earth turns, it looks as if the sun were setting.

When the Earth turns far enough, we cannot see the sun. Then we say it is night.

VIEW FROM SPACE ABOVE NORTH POLE

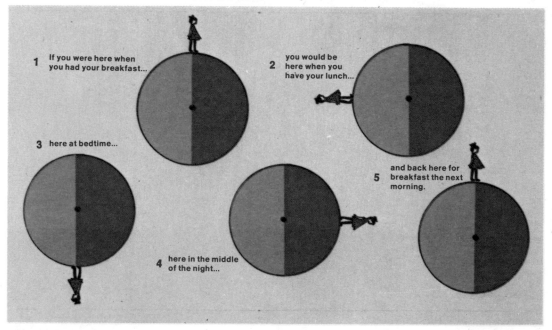

1 If you were here when you had your breakfast...

2 you would be here when you have your lunch...

3 here at bedtime...

5 and back here for breakfast the next morning.

4 here in the middle of the night...

When the Earth turns and we can see the sun, it is morning.

The Earth turns all the way around once in one day and one night.

You turn with the Earth, but you do not fall off. The Earth pulls you to it. This pull is called gravity.

Because of gravity we never feel upside down. "Down" points to the middle of the Earth. Your feet point down.

You do not feel yourself move as the Earth turns. That is because the air and everything around you turns with you.

The Earth turns as fast as most jets fly.

Some jets (like the Snowbirds) can match the Earth's turning speed— over 1,000 miles per hour!

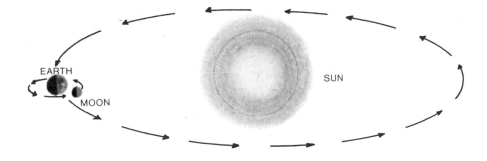

The Earth goes even faster in another way. It moves around the sun. The Earth takes the moon with it as it moves around the sun.

It takes Earth one year to go around the sun.

EARTH IS A PLANET

Because the Earth goes around the sun, the Earth is called a "planet." There are at least eight other planets that go around the sun, too. The nine planets are like one big family in the sky.

MERCURY

VENUS

EARTH

MARS

JUPITER

SATURN

URANUS

NEPTUNE

PLUTO

Saturn, photographed by *Voyager I* from 11 million miles away.

The other planets shine with the sun's light, just as the Earth and the moon do.

From Earth the planets look like stars in the sky. But stars twinkle. Planets do not.

Jupiter,
photographed by
Voyager I from
17.5 million
miles away.

Two planets, Venus and Mars, sometimes can be seen in the daytime.

At times stars and planets seem to have points on them. That is because we are looking at them through the air around the Earth.

Venus, photographed by *Mariner X* from 450,000 miles away.

Photographs of the red rock boulders on the surface of Mars were taken by *Viking II* which landed on Mars in 1976.

Stars in the Milky Way. Do you see the streak of light in the middle of the picture? This streak was made by a man-made satellite, *Echo I*. As it raced through space it heated up. The heat made it glow. It looked like a "shooting star".

"SHOOTING STARS"

A "shooting star" is not a real star. It is a bit of rock or stardust falling through space. It burns bright with the heat it makes as it passes through the air around the Earth.

WE NEED THE SUN, MOON, AND STARS

The sun gives us light and warmth. It helps plants grow and makes leaves green. The sun draws up water into clouds so it can rain again.

A space shuttle stands on its launch pad against the evening sky.
The space shuttle is the first spacecraft able to go into space and return to
Earth again and again. The first space shuttle, *Columbia,* flew in 1981.

The moon lights the Earth at night.

Planets and stars help pilots of ships and airplanes find their way at night.

All are wonderful to see.

WORDS YOU SHOULD KNOW

boil (BOYL) — the temperature at which water forms bubbles and steam is given off

bright (BRIYT) — give off much light; shine

Earth (ERTH) — the planet on which we live

flat — having a smooth, even surface; level

freeze — to change from a liquid to a solid

gravity (GRAV•ih•tee) — the force by which the Earth pulls other things toward its center

jet — an airplane which does not have a propeller and moves very fast

Mars — the planet which is fourth from the sun

mirror (MEER•er) — a smooth surface that reflects a picture of something

planet — a heavenly body which has no light of its own and which moves around the sun

rock — hard material which makes up the Earth

shooting star — material from outer space which burns and glows as it moves close to the Earth; meteor

space (SPAYS) — the area without end in which the stars and planets move

spacecraft (SPAYS•kraft) — a means of travel outside the Earth's atmosphere

spacemen (SPAYS•men) — people who travel in space

star — a body found in space which has its own light

sun — the star closest to the earth and around which the nine planets travel

trip — a journey; to travel

Venus — (VEE•nus) the planet which is second from the sun

INDEX

About the Author

Born in Gaston, Indiana, John Lewellen had a varied career in the communications field. He had been a newspaper reporter, author, and managing director for several radio and television programs. His lively interest in many things and rare talent for making a difficult subject easy to understand made his children's books very popular with young readers.